Snapdragons

Stage 8

Gill Howell

Teaching Notes

Contents

More Little Mouse Deer Tales

Jess and the Bean Root

Big Liam, Little Liam

The Band of Friends

Hair Scare

Raju's Ride

Introduction

The *Snapdragons* series is a rich mix of different kinds of stories presented as picture books with expertly written text carefully levelled to provide reading practice at each stage in Key Stage 1.

This set of six books at Stage 8 provides more challenging stories to encourage children to become confident readers. The stories have involved plots that reflect the feelings of the writer, with distinctive and rounded characters. They also provide further practice in reading key words, as well as useful vocabulary such as numbers and colour words, set in longer and more complex sentence structures.

The six books in Stage 8 include stories based in familiar settings that reflect everyday life, and the readers will quickly identify with the family members, school friends and pets, and recognise their experiences. There are different stories by the same author, animal fantasy tales, a retelling of a traditional nursery story with a new twist, and a set of three short animal trickster stories from another culture.

While mastering the longer texts, the children are still encouraged to look at the illustrations for visual cues to the words and to predict what is happening in the story. The picture book presentation will also encourage children to tell the story in their own words so that they develop their oral skills.

How to introduce the books

Before reading the story for guided or independent reading, always read the title and talk about the picture on the cover.

Go through the book together, looking at the pictures and talking about them. If there are context words (listed in the chart on page 4) that are new or unfamiliar, point them out and read them with the children. Read the story to the children, encouraging confident children to join in with you.

This booklet provides prompts and suggestions for using the books in groups and for guided, group and independent activities, matched to text, sentence and word level objectives. There are also separate Guided Reading Cards available for six titles at each stage. Suggestions are also provided for speaking and listening activities, writing activities, and cross-curricular links. You can use these suggestions to follow on from your reading or at another time.

Reading notes are also provided in each book. They can be found on the inside front and back covers of each book. These suggest friendly prompts and activities for parents or carers reading with their children at home.

Reading skills

Stage 8 develops:
- confident, independent reading
- awareness of more complex sentences
- awareness of more complex plots
- a readiness for conventional layout
- awareness of other viewpoints
- insights into feelings and motives of characters
- understanding of a wider range of stories.

Vocabulary chart

Stage 8		
More Little Mouse Deer Tales	Year 2 High frequency words	about again an as back be because been brother but by call called came can't could do don't down first from got had has have her here him his if jump(ed) just last laugh(ed) little made make may more much must next not now off one out over put ran saw sister so some than that them then there these time too tree very water way were what when where will with would
	Context words	mouse deer elephant forest trunk tiger dinner reflection gecko race
Jess and the Bean Root	Year 2 High frequency words	about after again an as back be because bed but by came could door down first from girl good got had help her here him his jump(ed) just little lived made more must name new night now off old one once out people put ran saw seen should so that them then there time too took very want way were what where will with your
	Context words	flats beanstalk bean castle balcony windows root tunnel cave Hugo friends
Big Liam, Little Liam	Year 2 High frequency words	about again an as back boy but call(ed) can't did do don't down first good got green had has have help her his house how if just laugh(ed) little live made make more name next night not now off one our out over people pull(ing) ran red saw so some take then that their them then there these time two very want were what who will with would your
	Context words	flat pizza Christmas cornflakes competition painting dragon prize award photographer tandem
The Band of Friends	Year 2 High frequency words	after again as back be but by could did door down first four from good had have here him his home how if jumped little live lived loved make more night not now off once one our out over put ran saw seen some that their then there three time too tree us very way were what when where white with would your
	Context words	cows ducks lambs sheep donkey dog cat rooster farmer noise adventure friends cottage robbers monster snake tiger crocodile eagle
Hair Scare	Year 2 High frequency words	about again as be bed but by came can't could don't down first from good got had have here him his home how if jump just laughed little make more much next night now off old one out over people put ran saw school so some than that there time too took very way want what when who with your Monday Wednesday Thursday Friday Saturday
	Context words	television moustache bathroom washroom cornflakes scissors hairdresser razor beard bald
Raju's Ride	Year 2 High frequency words	another back but came can't don't down first five four from got had have her here him his home house(s) jumped little lived loved made next not now off one our out people put ran saw school sister so take time their them then these three too took tree us very way were what when will with would your pink orange red yellow green white grey
	Context words	sandwich scooter ironing mango blanket peanuts parrots squirrels biscuits monkeys trousers samosa elephant

Curriculum coverage chart

Stage 8	Speaking and listening	Reading	Writing
More Little Mouse Deer Tales			
NLS/SLL	T4, Y2T3 24	T3, T4, S1, W3, W6	T12
Scotland	Level A/B	Level A/B	Level A/B
N. Ireland	Activities: a, b, c Outcomes: a, b, c, d, e	Activities: a, b, c, e Outcomes: b, c, d, e, f	Outcomes: a, b, c, e, i
Wales	Range: 1, 5 Skills: 2, 3, 4, 5	Range: 1, 2, 4, 5, 6 Skills: 1, 2	Range: 1, 2, 3, 6, 7 Skills: 1, 2, 3, 4, 5, 7, 8
Jess and the Bean Root			
NLS/SLL	Y2T3 24	T7, S1, W3, W6	T10
Scotland	Level A/B	Level A/B	Level A/B
N. Ireland	Activities: a, b, c Outcomes: a, b, c, d, e	Activities: a, b, c, e Outcomes: b, c, d, e, f	Outcomes: a, b, c, e, i
Wales	Range: 1, 5 Skills: 2	Range: 1, 2, 4, 5, 6 Skills: 1, 2	Range: 1, 2, 3, 6, 7 Skills: 1, 2, 3, 4, 5, 7, 8
Big Liam, Little Liam			
NLS/SLL	Y2T3 23	T3, S6, W1	T12
Scotland	Level A/B	Level A/B	Level A/B
N. Ireland	Activities: a, b, e, g Outcomes: a, c, d	Activities: a, b, c Outcomes: b, c, d, f	Outcomes: a, b, c
Wales	Range: 1, 3 Skills: 2, 3, 4, 5, 6	Range: 1, 2, 4, 5, 6 Skills: 1, 2	Range: 1, 2, 3, 6, 7 Skills: 1, 2, 3, 4, 5, 7, 8
The Band of Friends			
NLS/SLL	Y2T3 24	T3, S3, W8	T10
Scotland	Level A/B	Level A/B	Level A/B
N. Ireland	Activities: a, b, c Outcomes: a, b, c, d	Activities: a, b, c, e Outcomes: b, c, d, k	Outcomes: b, c, h, i
Wales	Range: 1, 2, 5 Skills: 1, 2, 3, 4, 5, 6	Range: 1, 2, 4, 5, 6 Skills: 1, 2	Range: 1, 2, 3, 6, 7 Skills: 1, 2, 3, 4, 5, 7, 8
Hair Scare			
NLS/SLL	Y2T3 23	T3, S2, W2, W4	T10
Scotland	Level A/B	Level A/B	Level A/B
N. Ireland	Activities: a, e, i Outcomes: a, b, c, d, f	Activities: a, b, c Outcomes: b, c, d, e, f	Outcomes: a, b, c, h, i
Wales	Range: 1, 2, 3 Skills: 1, 2, 3, 4, 5	Range: 1, 2, 4, 5, 6 Skills: 1, 2	Range: 1, 2, 3, 6, 7 Skills: 1, 2, 3, 4, 5, 7, 8
Raju's Ride			
NLS/SLL	Y2T3 24	T3, S4, W2, W4	T10
Scotland	Level A/B	Level A/B	Level A/B
N. Ireland	Activities: a, b, f, g, h Outcomes: a, b, g	Activities: a, b, c Outcomes: b, c, d, e, f	Outcomes: b, c, h, i
Wales	Range: 1, 2, 3 Skills: 1, 2, 3, 4, 5, 6	Range: 1, 2, 4, 5, 6 Skills: 1, 2	Range: 1, 2, 3, 6, 7 Skills: 1, 2, 3, 4, 5, 7, 8

More Little Mouse Deer Tales

Reading the story

Introducing the story

- Look together at the front cover, read the title and the author's name. Point out that these are tales from Malaysia, retold.
- Ask the children if they remember any other Little Mouse Deer Tales from their previous reading.
- Ask the children to suggest what sort of stories will be in the book.
- Ask them to look through the text and predict what will happen in the stories.

During reading

- Ask the children to read in a quiet voice as you listen to them individually.
- Praise the children when they read with confidence and self-correct on the run without prompting.
- Prompt the children to use different strategies to work out new words and make sense of their reading.
- Encourage the children to make use of punctuation, and words used to describe speech in place of 'said', in order to read expressively.

Observing Check that the children:
  - sustain their reading through each story and keep track of the plot.

Group and independent reading activities

Text level work

Range from another culture/different stories by same author

Objectives To notice the difference between spoken and written forms through re-telling known stories; compare oral versions with written text (T3); To compare books by same author: settings, characters, themes; to evaluate and form preferences, giving reasons (T4).

- Discuss the stories in this collection, and remind the children of the Little Mouse Deer story from stage 4, "Little Mouse Deer and the Crocodile". Ask the children: *What do all these stories have in common?*

- Ask the children to say which trick in the stories was best and why.
- Ask them to retell their favourite story in their own words to a partner. Ask the partner to find the story in the book, and identify any differences between the oral version and the written text.

Observing Are the children able to support their preferences by giving evidence from the story?

Sentence level work

Objective To read aloud with intonation and expression appropriate to the grammar and punctuation (S1).

- Ask the children to work with a partner and choose one of the stories in the collection.
- Encourage the children to read the dialogue, each taking the role of a character.
- Ask the children to read the words as they think each character would say them by noting the punctuation (question marks and exclamation marks), and any verbs that describe speech, e.g. "whispered", "shouted".
- Ask some of the pairs of children to read aloud for the class.

Observing Do the children accurately identify speech punctuation, and use the reporting clause to help them read expressively, e.g. "he said, rather crossly"; "cried Elephant", "she laughed".

Word level work

Objectives To discriminate, spell and read the phonemes _ear_ (hear) and _ea_ (head) (W3); To investigate words which have the same spelling patterns but different sounds (W6).

- Ask the children to turn to page 3 and put their finger on the word "heard".
- Write the vowels "ea" on the board. Ask the children to say the vowel sound in "heard" aloud.
- Ask the children if they can think of any other words with "ea" in them. Write their suggestions on the board and ask the children to say them aloud. Ask: _Do the vowels all sound the same?_
- Ask the children to search through the text and find any words with "ea" in them. Ask them to write the words on their whiteboards in groups of the same sounds. (heard; please/eat/leaves/screamed/beat; realised/nearby/really; head/ahead/already)

- Ask the children to suggest words with the same sound as "heard", e.g. "learn".

Observing Do the children scan the text to find the words? Are they able to hear the different vowel sounds?

Speaking and listening activities

Objectives To compare books by same author: settings, characters, themes; to evaluate and form preferences, giving reasons (T4); To present parts of traditional stories, own stories or work from different parts of the curriculum for members of their class (Y2T3 24).

- Ask the children to work in small groups and choose a story from the book.
- Get them to discuss together how to turn the story into a short play, and to rehearse it.
- Ask some of the groups to perform their play for the rest of the class.

Cross-curricular link
◀▶ PSHE: to take part in discussions with one person and the whole class

Writing

Objective To write simple evaluations of books read and discussed giving reasons (T12).

- Ask the children to write the title of the story they performed in the Speaking and listening activity (see above).
- Let the children write a paragraph describing why they chose it to present as a play.
- Ask the children to think about the characters, the dialogue and the setting, and to include how easy or difficult these were to put into their play.

Jess and the Bean Root
Reading the story
Introducing the story

- Look together at the front cover, read the title and the author's name.
- Ask the children to look closely at the cover illustration and read the title of the book Jess is reading.
- Ask the children to suggest what sort of story will be in the book.
- Ask them to look through the book at the illustrations to confirm their ideas.
- Identify any vocabulary which may be new or difficult for the children, e.g. p4 "balcony", "earth"; p8 "disappointed"; p12 "slippery"; p16 "friend".

During reading

- Ask the children to read in a quiet voice as you listen to them individually.
- Praise the children when they read with confidence and self-correct on the run without prompting.
- Prompt the children to use different strategies to work out new words and make sense of their reading.
- Encourage them to read the different print effects (bold print, speech bubbles, ellipsis) with appropriate expression, e.g. p16 "A.A..A...Atishoo!"

Observing Check that the children:
  - read with fluency, pausing only to check their reading makes sense of the story.

Group and independent reading activities
Text level work

Range new spin on traditional nursery tale/different stories by same author

Objective To compare books by different authors on similar themes; to evaluate, giving reasons (T7).

You will need a copy of "Jack and the Beanstalk" for reference.
- Ask the children to retell in their own words the story of "Jack and the Beanstalk". If necessary, tell them the story.

- Ask the children to say what is similar and different about "Jess and the Bean Root". Ask them to draw a grid with headings for four columns:

	Main character	Other characters	Setting	Plot
Jess and the Bean Root	Jess, a girl	Mum friendly giant	modern bean stalk	Jess slides down
Jack and the Beanstalk	Jack, a boy	Mum scary giant		

- Ask the children to work with a partner and to fill in details about "Jess and the Bean Root" and "Jack and the Beanstalk".
- Ask some of the children to say how "Jess and the Bean Root" is based on "Jack and the Beanstalk", giving evidence from the text.

Observing Do the children recognise similarities in the stories?

Sentence level work

Objective To read text aloud with intonation and expression appropriate to the grammar and punctuation (S1).

- Ask the children to work in groups of three.
- Get the children to read the dialogue, taking the roles of Jess, Mum and the giant.
- Ask the children to read the words as they think each character would say them by noting the punctuation (question marks and exclamation marks), and any verbs that describe speech, e.g. "shouted".
- Ask some of the groups of children to read aloud for the class.

Observing Do the children accurately identify speech punctuation?

Word level work

Objectives To discriminate, spell and read the phonemes *ear* (hear) and *ea* (head) (W3); To investigate words which have the same spelling patterns but different sounds (W6).

- Ask the children to turn to page 4 and put their finger on the word "bean".
- Write the vowels "ea" on the board. Ask the children to say the vowel sound in "bean" aloud.
- Ask the children to find the word "earth" and to say the vowel sound aloud.

- Ask the children to search through the text and find any words with "ea" in them. Ask them to write the words on their whiteboards in groups of the same sounds. (reading/bean/eating/hear/underneath; read/breakfast/heard)
- Ensure the children are aware of the different pronunciations for "read" (long vowel sound present tense) and "read" (short vowel sound past tense).

Observing Do the children scan the text to find the words? Are they able to hear the different vowel sounds?

Speaking and listening activities

Objective To present parts of traditional stories, own stories or work from different parts of the curriculum for members of their class (Y2T3 24).

- Ask the children to work in small groups and choose either "Jess and the Bean Root" or "Jack and the Beanstalk".
- Get the groups to discuss how to turn the story into a short play, and to rehearse it.
- Ask some of the groups to perform their play for the rest of the class.

Cross-curricular link
◀▶ Science: to recognise and name the leaf, flower, stem and root of flowering plants; that seeds grow into flowering plants.

Writing

Objective To write sustained stories, using their knowledge of story elements: narrative, settings, characterisation, dialogue and the language of story (T10).

- Discuss the elements of "Jess and the Bean Root" and "Jack and the Beanstalk" that the children identified for their charts (see Text level activity).
- Talk together about how to use the plots but add new characters and settings to plan a new story based on "Jack and the Beanstalk".
- Ask the children to add another row to their chart and make notes about the setting and plot.
- Encourage the children to think about the characters, and how they could be different from both Jess and the friendly giant, and Jack and the scary giant.
- Ask the children to use their notes to write a new story.

Big Liam, Little Liam

Reading the story

Introducing the story

- Look together at the front cover, read the title and the author's name. Ask the children to point out which boy is Big Liam and which is Little Liam.
- Turn to the title page. Ask the children to look at the illustration, and suggest what the story will be about.
- Ask the children to look through the book briefly at the illustrations to confirm their ideas.

During reading

- Ask the children to read in a quiet voice as you listen to them individually.
- Praise the children when they read with confidence and self-correct on the run without prompting.
- Prompt the children to use different strategies to work out new words and make sense of their reading.
- If necessary, provide the children with new difficult words (e.g. "confused", "competition"), so they don't struggle too long and lose the sense of the story.
- At the end of the story, ask the children: *Why do you think the author ended with the sentence "And they did!"?*

Observing Check that the children:
- read the high frequency words with confidence.

Group and independent reading activities

Text level work

Range language play/different story by same author

Objective To notice the difference between spoken and written forms through re-telling known stories; compare oral versions with the written text (T3).

- Ask the children to work with a partner and each take the role of one of the boys in the story.

- Ask the children to retell the story using the 1st person. Encourage them to add to the story by explaining how they feel about each other at different points in the story, and to explain why they kept their joint-painting a secret from their parents.
- Ask some of the pairs of children to perform their retellings for the class. Ask the class to say how these retellings are different from the written story.

Observing Are the children able to read between the lines? Do they infer that both Liams were pretending they might fall out if the other won the competition?

Sentence level work

Objective To turn statements into questions, learning a range of 'wh' words typically used to open questions: *what, where, when, who* and to add question marks (S6).

You will need a set of question words on cards for each pair of children.
- Ask the children to work with a partner.
- Turn the word cards upside down. Ask the children to take turns to pick a card, and then use the word to write a question about the story on their whiteboards.
- Tell the children to swap questions with their partner and answer the question orally.

Observing Do the children write their questions neatly, so that they can easily read each other's writing?

Word level work

Objective To secure phonemic spellings from previous 5 terms (W1).
- Ask the children to turn to page 2 and find the word "called" in the text. Ask them to say it aloud and listen closely to the "or" sound.
- Ask the children to find another word on the page with the same sound and spelling pattern. ("taller").
- Then ask them to find a third word on the page with the same sound, but with a different spelling pattern. ("Morden")
- Ask the children to search through the text and find any words with the "or" sound in them, and to write them on their whiteboards. ("ball", "caused", "morning", "talk")

- Encourage the children to suggest any other words with the same sound and spelling patterns from their own knowledge, and to write them under each word.
- Ask the children to practise spelling their lists using Look, Cover, Write and Check.

Observing Do the children scan the text to find the words? Are they able to recognise the vowel sounds?

Speaking and listening activities

Objective To work effectively in groups by ensuring each group member takes a turn, challenging, supporting and moving on (Y2T3 23).

- Write a question on the board: *Were Little Liam and Big Liam friends?*
- Ask the children to work in small groups, talk about how the boys in the story acted towards each other, and find evidence in the text to support their opinions.
- Encourage the children to think about how the boys acted towards their parents, e.g. Did they tease them?

Cross-curricular link
◀▶ PSHE: belonging to various groups and communities such as family and school

Writing

Objective To write simple evaluations of books read and discussed giving reasons (T12).

- Model how to write a book review for the class, using headings for them to use in their own writing, e.g. Title; Author; What the book is about; My favourite part; Who would enjoy reading this book.
- Ask the children to write their own review of the story.

The Band of Friends

Reading the story

Introducing the story

- Look together at the front cover, read the title and the author's name. Look together at the illustration. Ask the children to suggest what the story will be about and to identify the animals.
- Ask the children to look briefly through the book at the illustrations and confirm their ideas.
- Look at pages 4–5, and read the animal sounds together.
- Look at pages 16 and 21, and model how to read "AAAAA...h" and "Hisss..." in an expressive voice.
- Identify any new or unusual vocabulary for the children, e.g. p2 "contented", p10 "famished", p14 "delicious", p18 "refreshing".

During reading

- Ask the children to read in a quiet voice as you listen to them individually.
- Praise the children when they read with confidence and self-correct on the run without prompting.
- Praise the children when they read the animal sounds using an expressive voice.
- Prompt the children to use different strategies to work out new words and make sense of their reading.
- Encourage the children make use of punctuation, and words used to describe speech in place of "said", in order to read expressively, e.g. "sighed", "howled", "screamed".

Observing Check that the children:
- ■ make full use of the illustrations to help them if they struggle with some vocabulary.

Group and independent reading activities

Text level work

Range traditional story/from another culture/humorous/language play

Objective To notice the difference between spoken and written forms through retelling known stories; compare oral versions with written text (T3).

- Ask the children to think about how the story would be different if told by one of the animals, or one of the robbers.
- Let the children work with a partner, one taking the role of an animal, the other taking the role of a robber.
- Ask the children to tell each other the story aloud from their own point of view.
- Ask some of the pairs of children to describe how their retellings differ from each other, and from the written text.

Observing Are the children able to describe the story from a different viewpoint?

Sentence level work

Objective To use standard forms of verbs in speaking and writing, and to use past tense consistently for narration (S3).
- Read pages 4–5 together and identify all the verbs on the page.
- Model how to write the past tense verbs in one column, with a column adjacent for changing the tense to present, and then the present tense verbs in another column, with a column adjacent for changing the tense to past:
- Ask the children to change the tenses from past to present and vice versa.

past	present	present	past
loved		sing	

- Ask the children to identify which verbs do not have "–ed" endings when changed into the past tense.

Observing Can the children identify irregular past tense verbs, e.g. sang/sing, heard/hear, was/is?

Word level work

Objective To secure understanding and use of the terms "vowel" and "consonant" (W8).
- Ask the children to turn to pages 4–5 and say how the animals felt about their singing.
- Ask the children to find the word "proud" on the page and say the "ou" vowel sound.

- Encourage the children to search through the text and find any other words with the same spelling in them and write them on their boards.
- Ask the children to group the words according to their different sounds (e.g. proud/loud/shouted/our/counting/out/ground; could/would; group/through/famous/four).
- Ask the children to practise spelling the words using Look, Cover, Write and Check.

Observing Do the children scan the text to find the words? Are they able to hear the different vowel sounds?

Speaking and listening activities

Objective To present parts of traditional stories, own work or work from different parts of the curriculum for members of their class (Y2T3 24).

- Ask the children to work in small groups and discuss how to turn the story into a short play, then to rehearse it.
- Ask some of the groups to perform their play to the rest of the class.

Cross-curricular link
◀▶ PSHE: to take part in discussions with one person and the whole class

Writing

Objective To write sustained stories, using their knowledge of story elements: narrative, settings, characterisation, dialogue and the language of story (T10).

- Discuss the settings of the story with the children: the beginning (farm); the middle (wood); the ending (cottage).
- Model how to write the settings onto a story map.
- Ask the children to say who the characters were in the story, and model how to write them onto the story map.
- Ask the children to use the story map as a basis for writing the story in their own words.

Hair Scare

Reading the story

Introducing the story

- Look together at the front cover, read the title and the author's name.
- Ask the children to look at the illustration and suggest what might happen in the story.
- Get the children to look through the book at the illustrations to confirm their ideas.
- Ask the children to turn to pages 4–5, and find the word "moustache" in the text.

During reading

- Ask the children to read in a quiet voice as you listen to them individually.
- Praise the children when they read with confidence and self-correct on the run without prompting.
- Prompt the children to use different strategies to work out new words and make sense of their reading.
- On pages 8–9, encourage the children to read Jamie's spoken words "But it **is** real!" with expression. Explain that the author begins Jamie's words with "But" so it sounds like real conversation.
- On pages 10–11, ask the children to read the two sentences at the start of the second paragraph "He had to lift…. And when…". Ask them to reread them, omitting the word "And". Ask: *What effect does using "And" have at the beginning of this sentence?*
- On page 11, if the children have difficulty reading "scissors", ask them to predict the word by looking at the illustration.

Observing Check that the children:
  - make use of the punctuation to read with expression.

Group and independent reading activities

Text level work

Range humorous/extended story

Objective To notice the difference between spoken and written forms through re-telling known stories; compare oral versions with written text (T3).

- Ask some of the children to take the role of Jamie and to sit in the hot seat.
- Ask the other children to question Jamie about what happened to him in the story. Encourage them to ask about Jamie's feelings.
- Ask the children to say what was different about the story as told by "Jamie" in the hot seat.

Observing Do the children recognise the change from a third person account to a first person recount?

Sentence level work

Objective The need for grammatical agreement, matching verbs to nouns/pronouns; using simple gender forms e.g. *his/her* correctly (S2).
You will need the following sentences from the story, and pronouns, written on the board:

Jamie was in a bad mood.
Mum got the scissors.
Mrs Moore said.
By Wednesday morning, the moustache had grown over Jamie's mouth.
Jamie and Laura had to send for Mrs Moore to come out.
Dad managed to shave off one side of the moustache.
He, She, They, it, his, her

- Ask the children to rewrite the sentences, changing the underlined nouns into pronouns.

Observing Do the children read their rewritten sentences, to check they make sense?

Word level work

Objectives To reinforce work on discriminating syllables in reading and spelling from previous term (W2); To secure reading and spelling of the high frequency words in Appendix List 1 (W4).

- Ask the children to look through the text and find the names of the days of the week in the story. Ask: *Which two days are missing?* (Tuesday and Sunday)
- Ask the children to clap the syllables of the words as they say them aloud.
- Ask the children to write the words down and to practise spelling them using Look, Cover, Write and Check.

● Ask: *Which two words have three syllables?*

Do the children scan the text to find the words?

Speaking and listening activities

Objective To work effectively in groups by ensuring each group member takes a turn, challenging, supporting and moving on (Y2T3 23).

● Ask the children to work in small groups and discuss any changes they think will improve their group stories (see Writing activity below), e.g. adding dialogue, choosing more powerful words to express feelings.
● Encourage the children to read their stories aloud within their group, and to rewrite where they have made group decisions about changes.
● Ask the groups to rehearse reading their polished stories.
● Ask some of the groups to read their story aloud for the rest of the class.

Cross-curricular link
◀▶ PSHE: to take part in discussions with one person and the whole class

Writing

Objective To write sustained stories, using their knowledge of story elements: narrative, settings, characterisation, dialogue and the language of story (T10).

● Discuss the events of the story with the class, and on the board write: *Beginning, Middle, Ending.*
● Model how to make notes about these parts of the story on the board.
● Ask the children to work in small groups of three or four, and discuss what they would put in a story, written by the group, about dreaming they grew a moustache.
● Ask the group to decide which part of the story to write, and to each make notes about what the group wants to happen in the story.
● Ask each child to write their own part of the story, then read it to the group.
● When the children are happy with their group story, ask some of them to read it aloud for the rest of the class.

Raju's Ride

Reading the story

Introducing the story

- Look together at the front cover, read the title and the author's name.
- Ask the children to look at the cover illustration, and the title page, and suggest where the story is set.
- Encourage the children to look through the book at the illustrations to confirm their ideas.
- Ask the children: *What do you think will happen in the story?*

During reading

- Ask the children to read in a quiet voice as you listen to them individually.
- Prompt the children to use different strategies (break words into smaller chunks, reread and predict words that make sense and check the illustrations) to work out new words and make sense of their reading.
- On page 2, ask: *What does the author mean by "were like the filling in a sandwich"?*
- Ask: *What do the words from the scooter show?*
- Praise the children when they read with confidence and self-correct on the run without prompting.
- As the children read, occasionally ask them to tell you what is happening in their own words, to ensure they understand the story.

Observing Check that the children:
- ■ make use of the punctuation to read dialogue with expression.

Group and independent reading activities

Text level work

Range from another culture/extended story

Objective To notice the difference between spoken and written forms through re-telling known stories; compare oral versions with the written text (T3).

- Ask the children to look through the story and make notes of what Raju did when he delivered the ironing.
- Ask the children to use the notes as a prompt to retell the story to a partner.
- Let the children look through the written story and find where their retellings differed.

Observing Do the children include relevant detail in their note-taking, e.g. writing colours, names?

Sentence level work

Objective To use commas in lists (S4).

You will need a sentence starter written on the board: Raju was given...

- Ask the children to look through the text, find all the gifts and complete the sentence.

Observing Do the children use commas to separate the items Raju was given in their sentence? Do they include details from the story, and end with a full stop?

Word level work

Objectives To reinforce work on discriminating syllables in reading and spelling from previous term (W2); To secure reading and spelling of all the high frequency words in Appendix List 1 (W4).

- Ask the children to look through the text and find the names of the colours in the story. (pink, orange, red, yellow, grey, green, white)
- Ask the children to clap the syllables of the words as they say them aloud.
- Ask them to look at the illustrations and add any other colour words to the list from their own knowledge.
- Encourage the children to write the words down and to practise spelling them using Look, Cover, Write and Check.

Observing Do the children scan the text to find the words?

Speaking and listening activities

Objective To present parts of traditional stories, own stories or work from different parts of the curriculum for members of their class (Y2T3 24).

- See the Writing activity below. Ask the children to discuss Raju's character. Prompt them to think about what Raju did with each of the gifts he was given.
- Ask the children to suggest a "moral" for the end of the story, e.g. "good deeds are rewarded".
- Ask the children to use their completed story plans as a prompt to tell the story aloud for the class, using their own words.

Cross-curricular link
◀▶ PSHE: belonging to various groups and communities such as family and school

Writing

Objective To write sustained stories, using their knowledge of story elements: narrative, settings, characterisation, dialogue and the language of story (T10).

- Discuss the setting and events of the story with the class.
- Draw a story plan on the boards, e.g.

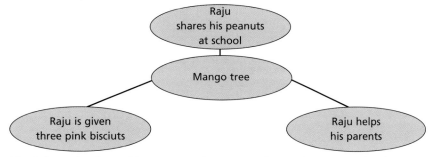

- Model on the board how to make notes about the events in the story.
- Ask the children to draw their own story plan and add bubbles to the diagram to organise their story.
- Ask the children to write the story in their own words using their diagrams as a prompt.
- When they are happy with their story, ask some of them to read it aloud for the rest of the class.

Oxford Reading Tree resources at this level

There is a range of material available at a similar level to these stories which can be used for consolidation or extension.

Stage 8

Teacher support
- Teacher's Handbook
- Guided reading Cards for Stage 8 Stories
- Take-Home Card for each story
- BBC Storytapes + Teacher's Activity Book
- Stage 8 Workbooks 1–3
- Woodpeckers Photocopy Masters
- Group Activity Sheets Book 3 Stages 6–9
- ORT Games Stages 6–9

Further reading
- Oxford Reading Tree Storybooks for Core Reading
- Stage 8 Playscripts
- Woodpeckers Phonics Anthologies 6–7
- Robins (for extended reading practise)
- Jackdaws Anthologies
- Fireflies Non-Fiction
- ORT True Stories (narrativer non-fiction)
- Fact Finders Units E-F
- Story Rhymes
- Glow-worms Poetry

Electronic
- Clip Art
- Stage 6 & 7 Talking Stories
- ORT Online www.OxfordReadingTree.com
- Floppy and Friends

OXFORD
UNIVERSITY PRESS

Great Clarendon Street, Oxford OX2 6DP

Oxford University Press is a department of the University of Oxford. It furthers the University's objective of excellence in research, scholarship, and education by publishing worldwide in

Oxford New York

Auckland Cape Town Dar es Salaam Hong Kong Karachi Kuala Lumpur Madrid Melbourne Mexico City Nairobi New Delhi Shanghai Taipei Toronto

With offices in

Argentina Austria Brazil Chile Czech Republic France Greece Guatemala Hungary Italy Japan Poland Portugal Singapore South Korea Switzerland Thailand Turkey Ukraine Vietnam

Oxford is a registered trade mark of Oxford University Press in the UK and in certain other countries

© Oxford University Press 2005

The moral rights of the author have been asserted

Database right Oxford University Press (maker)

First published 2005

British Library Cataloguing in Publication Data

Data available

Series adviser Shirley Bickler

Cover illustration Stephen Waterhouse

Teacher's Notes: ISBN 978 0 19 8455677

10

Page make-up by Fakenham Photosetting, Fakenham, Norfolk

Printed in China by Imago